C000185615

The Secret Garden of My Heart

Poems and Drawings
William C Denning

Pomegranate
BOOKS

To my wife Gill, my children and grandchildren

Acknowledgements:

Gill Denning would like to express her sincere thanks to Jan Keene and Gill Kibble for all the painstaking work they put into the compilation and editing of this volume.

Maypole Farm, the home of William and Gill Denning

First published in 2007

Copyright © Gill Denning 2007

ISBN 978-1-84289-011-0

Printed in Great Britain by
The Good News Press, Ongar, Essex

Published by Pomegranate Books
3 Brynland Avenue, Bristol BS7 9DR
www.pomegranatebooks.co.uk

CONTENTS

THE SECRET GARDEN
OF MY HEART

The Secret Garden of My Heart

In the secret places
of my waiting longing heart
teach me eternal wisdom
show me holy love

In the still and quiet places
of my waiting aching heart
I move into a secret garden
in the evening summer light
and sense a haunting awesome fragrance
call me on

I take this gift of time
to touch the trees and breathe the flowers
and listen to the gently moving wind
and feel the sun's warmth on my watchful face

I take the time to find the hidden pool
itself a secret in this secret place

Slowly deeply calmly
I will look into the pool
and see the mirrored shadow
and the darkness in the shadow
and in the darkness
all the hidden wounds that bleed unseen

I take the time to look into my eyes
my own dark eyes
reflecting back a sadness
driven by anguished childhood pain

I choose to see beyond
the shadowed image of my wounded self
and dare to see within my eyes
the eyes of One
who knows all things
and looks at me with gentle caring love
and all the splendid wisdom of eternity
        that knows all things
        that sees all things

and understands all things
and therefore looks with love

And as I let love's wisdom
touch the dark and wounded places of my soul
I know and feel that true unchanging love
        forgive the most destructive sins
        and heal the self-inflicted wounds
        and set me free to be at peace
        to walk with freedom and with joy
within the secret garden of my heart

So teach me wisdom teach me love
within the secret garden of my heart

A Candle Burns

A candle burns
when the day is long and hard
A candle burns
and says
I will keep faith with you
When the fears bite deep
and your soul is torn
with doubt
and your mind shuts out the pain
that will not
cannot be shut out
know this:

A candle burns
that asks no thing from you
save that you feel its warmth
and that you find its gentle light
is stronger
than the darkness of the night

Know this:
that flame
will never never die

FINCHALE
PRIORY

God My Maker

Thou hast said, 'Seek ye my face'
My face says to thee, 'Thy face, Lord, do I seek'

Psalm 27: 8

God my Maker you have said 'seek my face'
With my heart and all I feel I seek your face
      Sorrow and joy
      anger and fear
      dreaming and hope
await your healing touch within my wounded heart

God my Maker you have said 'seek my face'
With my soul and all I am I seek your face
      Darkness and light
      yearning and faith
      aching desire
await your healing touch within my longing soul

God my Maker you have said 'seek my face'
With my mind and all I think I seek your face
      Anguish and pain

   disquiet and stress
   confusion and doubt
await your healing touch within my struggling mind

God my Maker you have said 'seek my face'
With my strength and all I do I seek your face
   Stillness and movement
   working and playing
   passion and sensing
await your healing touch upon my striving strength

God my Maker you have said 'seek my face'
With heart and soul, with mind and strength
   I search and find
   and see you in the One
   whose hands and feet are torn
   whose way is truth
   whose truth is life
   and in this face of Christ
   I see your love that calls me on
   beyond the end of time

The Butterfly

Batter your fragile wings
O little one
against unyielding glass
called on by golden light
and gentle warmth
called on by burning love
to leave the cold dark prison
where your soul
is frozen locked and safe
and where your heart
is chilled and held unmoved
where buried feelings lie
untouched unheard
and wait the call to be
to feel
to grow
to fly
to float upon the wind

and drink pure honey
from a hundred glorious flowers
and taste
the fierce sharp pain
of freedom's ecstasy
and all the risk of heaven
and deepest hell

The long dark winter waiting time
has gone
and you must leave
the murky refuge
where your soul was locked away
unseen
unknown
and where your brilliant shining wings
held close and darkly shadowed
in the place where no light shines
or movement stirs
can feel a vibrant quickening in the depths

But now your soul is touched
by gentle light
that burns and heals
and burns again
and flames the shadowed colours
of your folded wings
that open to a glory
you have never known
nor dared believe
and there is no return

The chill night's frost
and daylight's predators
will always wait
the fragile moment
when your heart is weak
and strength is low
and will has gone
and you will search again
the safety of your prison shell

and long to fold your wings
and slip away into the darkness
of a numb oblivion

Then
and then
you must
you can
you will
batter your wings
against unyielding glass
and wait the gentle hand
itself so deeply scarred
with nails and thorns
that lifts the catch

Then you are free to fly with angel's wings
beyond the demon's grasp
And far beyond that grasp
the chalice waits
held by those same scarred hands

and you are free to drink
the sacred wine of heaven
where every waiting flower shall be that cup
the holy cup
that feeds your aching thirsting soul
with costly healing love

The bread and wine of heaven
the brilliant shining wings
that lift you high

The choice
the awesome choice
the love that heals

All these are yours
all yours that you may live

Batter your fragile wings
courageous little one
and you will live

TORTWORTH
11/06/02
W.C.D.

I Meet You Holy One

I meet You Holy One
in the mystic shadowed places
of the forest depths
and find a gentle water's edge
beyond the bounds
of human space and time
where words give way to silence
and where search gives way
to stillness
and the struggling hurting mind
lets go the desperate need
for knowledge
answers
certainty and truth
and finds
a deeper inner knowing
far beyond the grasp of thought
or sense's touch

where love
pure holy love
has crossed the boundaries
of my wounds and needs
and set me free

To the Rest of the World

To the rest of the world
         you said
         I'm solid and comfortable

To you
         you said
         I feel like a gaping hole

Hear this my friend
today and every day
I hold that gaping hole
you choose to share with me
in tender caring love across the space

And I would gently touch
that dark torn hole
which sometimes feels like death
and share the pain
within your human heart
the pain that is

the counterpoint of life
the other side of light and hope and peace
  the searing pain
  that interweaves with ecstasy
  the sorrow on the shadow side of joy
that all must feel
who choose to face their inner longing need
and reach towards
the hidden mysteries
  and can not
  can not have
  and can not be

Remember this:

today and every day
we hold those aching wounds
we choose to share
in tender caring love across the space

In the Depths of my Heart

In the depths of my heart
there is a burning love for you O Holy One
beyond understanding
explanation
reason

But also in my heart there are wounds
that twist the way I live
that reason knows
and knowledge understands
but will and will alone cannot control

O God I would you had my wholeness
not my wounds
for there is wholeness there

Would that I had my love to give
and not my brokenness
for that love is there

A Meditation on the Mystery of Love

I felt the sound of angels' wings
and heard a silent whisper
in the darkness of the night
and for a moment
knew beyond all knowing
who I am
when shaped by pain and love
by love and pain

Sorrow and joy and love
join gentle wounded hands
and banish fear
but can not will not should not
banish pain
when all that fear had grasped
had been let go

The deepest wounds that bleed
in quiet stillness

far beyond the edge of measured time
are held within the heart of One
whose name is Love
And here I dare to touch the mystery
of broken bread and wine
that waits and waits
within eternity
and feels the emptying
that asks for nothing in return

Then comes the unsought gift
on angels' wings
the gift of peace that always waits within the depths
to hear the call of love
and reaches out to meet and touch the grief
till all the tearing ugliness
of unacknowledged pain
is whole and clean
For pain alone
can measure love's intensity

within the awesome silence of Your love

And in this place
beyond the edge of measured space and time
there is an ecstasy more near to tears
for here I know and I am known
and in that inner knowing
of my darkness and my light
I find the One
who never for one moment
had lost me

The Wye Valley

Today
the sun shone
misty
subdued
haunting
beautiful
and the Wye Valley trees
sang silent songs
joyful and sad
full of deep mystery
yearning and longing
till the tears came
slowly

Lost and found
in the dark green forest depths
in my heart
in my soul

Today
my heart leaped up
and flamed with painful joy
in the dark green forest depths
and always will

You Called Me

Before I formed you in the womb I knew you,
and before you were born I consecrated you...
Behold I have put my words in your mouth.

Jeremiah 1 : 5, 9

So you called me
before I was born you say
You had ideas for me
before my mind could think
or dreams could play their games
or wild imaginings
could stir my childish hope

I understand that you called Moses
from the burning bush
with clear commands
to set your people free

And that you called Elijah
on the mountain
not in earthquake wind or fire

but with your still small voice

And that you called Mary
waiting
filled with awesome dread
to bear your son

But these are awesome moments
in our time
and yet beyond our time
Moses Elijah Mary
Can I believe that you called me
before my infant heart could feel
before my mind could know
my lips could speak
my eyes could see
before my tiny half-formed hands
could touch and hold

Can I believe O Christ
that you have need of me

to be your heart
to feel the screaming pain of those
whose lives touch mine

Can I believe
that you have need of me
to be your hands
to touch the wounded broken ones
whose lives are torn by fear and need and pain

Can I believe
that you have need of me
to be your mouth
to speak your healing words
of love and peace and hope
to those who know no love
no peace
no hope

Can I believe
that you have need of me

to be your ears
to hear the cry of broken hearts
that ache for love

The timeless ageless Christ
confronts me with this truth:
Before you were formed in the womb
I loved you and knew you
and before you were born
I had chosen you
and now
I have put my words in your mouth
my love in your heart
and my hands are your hands
and your hands are my hands

I do not ask you to be special
with your gifts or beautiful
or clever with your words
or strive for great success

I ask of you just this
Come follow me
with faith and hope and love

Come follow me

When the Night is Dark

When the night is dark
and the pain bites deep
        I will keep faith
        for you

When you feel alone
and far from home
and the soft warm lights
mock your bleeding soul
        I will keep faith
        with you

When the demons scream
their bitter words
and spit
their poisoned venom to destroy
        I shall keep faith

There is a depth
beyond the pain
a still mysterious depth
where I will hold you
with my faith
my love
my hidden inner knowing
that is silent
still and strong
        I will keep faith
        I will

Be Still

And a voice strange and beautiful said

Be still
be still and know
first be still breath softly gently
in the dark
and know that you are loved
with love beyond all knowing
love stronger than death
is my love
deeper than your darkness
holding your demons ghosts and witches
holding till they are healed
or they are you

Let go
breathe gently
till the darkness is your womb
Ghosts witches demons

healed
all healed
are angels in your soul

There Is a Solemn Stillness in My Soul

There is a solemn stillness in my soul
that walks alone
alone by choice
to tread a forest path
which neither I
nor any feet have trod before

Sorrow and sadness
wash my aching love with gentle tears
and hidden wounds bleed softly
in the welcome covering darkness of the starlit night

Alone
yet not alone
for in the shadow of your wings O Holy One
I wait in hope

Dear mother God
you know it all
and with your tender eyes

you saw my wounded truth
before my birth
and with your waiting love
you watched me struggle through the years
and saw my wounded wounding pain-filled search

An empty aching
unfulfilled
that left me gasping
shuddering
with bitter angry pain upon a distant lonely shore
In the shadow of your wings O Holy One
I wait in hope

I Give You Thanks for All She Was

O God who was made known to me when I began
within my mother's care
I give you thanks for all she was
her broken flesh that grew me
and her broken heart that loved me
her empty breasts that fed me
when she could not feed herself
and for her aching arms that held me
when she could not hold herself
and for her wounded soul that showed me Christ
when faith had all but vanished in her depths

For suffering love
and anguished care
that met my needs
when life was bleak
and all within her screamed
with inner turmoil torn by guilt and shame
I give you thanks

And in that heartfelt painful gratitude
I reach towards her
where she rests in peace
to hold her in my arms
and wash her with my tears
and heal her with my love

For I have come to know
her love
her deep and special love
that held me
even when I turned away in fear

For I have come to trust her arms
her gentle arms
that held me
even when I pushed her touch away alarmed

For I have come to know so much
so much
that I am overwhelmed by grief

and guilt sometimes
that I had hurt her so

So late
but not too late
for grace on angels' wings
to carry
what I think and say and feel
to where she is beyond the edge of space and time

So may her loving soul
find peace at last
that life denied
and be at rest in Christ

Amen

Such Deep and Poignant Sadness

Such deep and poignant sadness
fills my heart and mind
and fills my soul
with aching yearning tears
that come from distant places
distant times

I am a child again
a little crying boy
who wants his mum
and she has gone
was always gone
too deep
within her own bleak screaming pain
to hear my infant need
and take me to her self
and keep me safe
from nightmare demons
hiding in the dark

And through the years
some hard and painful years
I searched for you
and longed for you
and needed you
to hold me close
and make me safe
and feed me
from your warm full breasts
your skin against my skin
my hand in yours

I searched for you
reached out to touch you
where you were not
could not be

I clung to darkness
and therefore
could not touch you
when you needed touch

and could not hold you
when you needed love

I could not be there
when your heart cried out
'forgive'
until I had forgiven
your milkless breasts
your tired angry words
your push away
that sent me into hell
a bitter angry hell
that fed resentment
through my growing years
and caused
a deadly bleeding wound
within my depths
and built a high harsh wall
within my heart
a wall I could not

would not climb
that kept me from you
and denied
that closeness
longed by me
and sought by you

Until
that day when darkness
yielded to the power of light
and I could say
forgive me
for the years of bitter hurt
forgive
the nurtured angry wound
within my heart
from childhood pain and fear
that did not
could not understand
your pain your fear

your deep
and angry wounds
unseen
unknown
unhealed
that tore the tender fabric
of your soul
which then tore mine

Then light
forgiving light
pure healing light
shone through my darkened soul
and I could touch you
hold you
love you
without fear

Such deep and poignant sadness
fills my heart and mind
and fills my soul
when I reflect
that healing took so long

St. Nicholas, Cholmondeley ham 98.

Quietly You Went Last Night
A poem for Lilian Mary Denning 1902-1997

Quietly
you went last night
not raging
at life's pain
and childhood wounds
that tore your inner secret life
and stole your infant dreams
before those dreams could be

Quietly you went
into the darkness of the night
and far beyond that darkness
to a mystic golden light
where dawn was gently breaking
on another day
another world
beyond the feeble grasp
of struggling finite minds

so clever yet so blind
that seek in vain to understand
the mystery of life
and death
and God

Quietly you went
into the darkness of the night
and far beyond
but not beyond the reach
of human love
our love
and yours
and not beyond the reach
of memory
of joy of pain
both yours and ours

For we shall talk of you
and think of you
again

and share the stories
that will ache our hearts
and we shall laugh and cry
until a quiet stillness
fills the silent space
where words must end

Quietly you went
into the darkness of the night
and far beyond
your footsteps light
way past the hidden edge
of space and time
where souls' wings softly meet
and touch each other's wings
and whisper
soundless words of welcome
healing words of love
to meet your journey's end
with songs of joy

And you
caught up at last
and safe for ever
with the One
whose name is Love

Quietly you went
into the darkness of the night
and far beyond

60

We Watched You Fly

Written following the funeral of my mother, after watching a flock
of geese flying overhead

We watched you fly
low across the dark November sky
washed with a gentle rain
that cried with us
though not with anguished grief
nor ugly pain

For this was memory time
and listening time
and story-telling time
and we had come to say goodbye
and tears were not of anguished grief
nor ugly pain

We watched you fly low
and brilliant white
against a blue black sky

with wonder and with joy
we watched you
beat your angel wings
with gentle grace
and hold your haloed heads
with dignity

And did you see us see you
fly away
across those autumn skies
towards a glorious secret sunset
hidden by the clouds
your unseen path prepared
by angels gone before
to wait with love
at heaven's gate
to bring you to your home
within our hearts

And home at last
your wounds all healed

your scars transformed
your heavy dragging footsteps
drag no more
for you can leap and run and fly
beyond the stars
within our hearts
your pain all gone
and you are young again

We watched you fly low
across the dark November sky
washed with a gentle rain
and said goodbye

Ashe Parish Churchyard

Reflections on a visit Gill and I made to my home,
where I grew up.

They lay here
my parents
where we had said goodbye
deep in the winter earth at Ashe
amongst the headstones
close to Norah
close to Bert

The silent gentle churchyard knew it all
had seen it all
through centuries of timeless time
as each grave
received the tired gift
that set souls free
from harsh unyielding pain
or took a tiny struggling life
its future torn away

by harsh disease
or cruel plague
or grinding poverty

We stood there quiet
hearts and minds
attentive
listening
still
the winter weather mild
and edged with chill

I sensed with awe
this memory place
this church and farm
where I
a longing little child
soulful
near to God
had played
and prayed

in solitude
and cried and dreamed a way
into the torment of my teenage years

We walked
reflective
thoughtful
to the railway arch
where we had walked
so many times
a hundred years before
when we were young
the future
all unknown
our children
all unborn
our stories
all untold

Looking back
beyond the parish church
beyond the farm
from way across the fields at Berrydown
the evening sun
low in the darkening sky
shone through the leafless trees
edging the heavy clouds
with flaming joy
flooding a golden light
across the naked stubble
and the bare brown earth
and making winter hedgerows
glow and sing
before the all-consuming night
would gather up this gold
and one more precious day
could die
and rest in peace

After France

Abbeys and forests
darkly mystical
haunting and beautiful
enrich my solitude
with pain and joy

The abbey's vaulted nave
that holds me
flooded with mystery
echoes back the silent music
of time before time
and beyond
where there is peace

The forest's haunting depths
darkness and light
that call me on
to search tomorrow's hidden paths
to trust the darkness

and believe the gentle light

For there will always be
the abbey
the forest
each holds the darkness and the light

The Early Morning Sun

Beautiful images - churches, winter trees and the light- all some-
how get right through to me and make me so deeply sorrowful, as
if they touch some hidden well of grief.

The early morning sun
shines low
flooding the winter trees
with golden light
and I am sad
to see that light
and feel it
touch some deeply hidden
secret well of unheard grief
that spreads such sorrow
through the silent stillness
of the landscape of my soul
where none have been
and only I shall walk
alone

in solitude
and choose to touch that grief
and choose to feel that swelling sadness
ache my wounded heart
that fills my mind with images
and icons
from my yesterdays
that haunt tomorrow's trackless journey
in the forest's depths
where I must be at one
with who I am
and feel the grief
and bear the pain
and grow beyond the darkness
to the peace
that also hides within my secret depths
where I am one with God
whose name is Love

A Stable in South Gloucestershire.   WCD 2003

For Those Whose Lives I Touch

O God dear God
what mystery waits
when we can learn to leave behind
the tawdry search
for meaning pleasure purpose
goal or strength
for might and power
for love
for wealth
for things
when all has been let go
and we stand naked in the rain
that washes all this pointless emptiness away

From the fullness of my heart
I see my wounded sisters brothers
I see them search
I see them steal
I see them fight

What can I give
though not a gift
that gives back only in return

Reaching out to others
from this holy place of peace
surrounded by my trees and stone and wood
could sound pretentious arrogant
the wanderings of an ageing man

There is a love
for those whose lives I touch
and want for them
the peace that I have found

I want for them
a sort of inner wholeness
which all humanity must long for
seek
and one day surely must
will find

You Lie Hidden in the Depths

Truly, thou art a God who hidest thyself

Isaiah 45:15

God my Maker you have said 'seek my face'
your face I seek
but you lie hidden in the depths
beyond imagination's reach
or sense or thought

Feeling alone can touch the mystery
as awe and wonder
fear and dread
delight and joy
join hands
and take me to the place where
no paths lie
and none have ever been before

And here within these mystic forest depths
where I must walk alone

I meet the One
whose hands are torn
whose face is scarred whose feet still bleed
whose burning eyes shall see beyond
      the masks I wear to hide my fear
      the games I play to win approving love
whose listening ears shall hear beyond
      the stammering words I speak to hide my shame
      the half true lies I use to win control
whose gentle voice shall speak
      with quiet strength
      to call me near and draw me close
whose touch shall heal
      the secret hidden wounds
      that some can see and yet I will not
      dare not name

Silent and still within my aching heart
I walk with courage and with hope
into the unknown darkness of the forest depths

where sometimes
      no birds sing
      and threatening demons hide
      and seek to break my longing heart
      and tear my quiet soul
and other times
this mystic forest place
      is filled with blazing golden light
      birds sing their glorious songs
      and angels wait with bread and wine from
      heaven
      to feed my starving soul
      and give me life again

I choose to walk into the unknown place
of darkness or of light
to seek your face
and trust to meet the One
who sees and hears and speaks with flaming love
and waits with healing touch to make me whole

The Forest's Stillness

Between the forest's stillness
and the silence of the pool
and beyond the winter's darkness
waits a gentle spring

At the end of movement
stillness waits
and breathes a healing calm

At the end of words
silence speaks
and whispers quiet peace

The Mystery of Love and Suffering
Watching the film 'Schindler's List' raised all the old questions

And while I slept
a thousand million years
had whispered past and
who am I
to dream of meaning
destiny and truth

I am such fragile living breathing dust
locked for a moment
or a thousand years
in space and time
who thinks and feels
who knows and loves
who hates and fears
who thinks he thinks
and feels he feels
and knows
but does not know

and rages
at the mystery
of love
and suffering
and God

And when the rage
has for a moment gone
and peace returns
unanswered questions
wait their time

For they will come again
to rock and shake
my slender grasp of meaning
truth
and life

When I reflect on Him
whose way was love
whose truth was life

I see a suffering crucifix
within the heart of God

And every newborn child
who walks this earth
must bear that image too
within their heart

And they may dare
to choose
to live this way
and find this truth
that all life's glorious joy
is touched with searing pain
and all life's hideous pain
is touched with living hope
and all life's dismal failure
chosen wrong
is touched with healing love
when I reflect on Him
whose way

whose truth
whose life
was joy and pain and love

The Fruit of the Spirit
The fruit of the Spirit is love, joy, peace...
Galatians 5: 22

Come healing Spirit
to my darkening night
and liberate
the love that waits
to touch the self-inflicted wounds
that bleed unhealed

Come healing Spirit
to my darkening night
and liberate
the joy that waits
to flame up in my aching heart
and blaze with glorious fire

Come healing Spirit
to my darkening night
and liberate
the peace that waits
within my burdened soul
and set my longing spirit free

The Dragonfly Emerges from the Pond

Tremble your glistening wings
break free from predators and slime
that cling
unfeeling of your need
imprisoning and dark

Tremble your glistening wings
and let the sun's bright warmth
bring freedom from the world
you knew
and have outgrown

Dangers wait
and yet more urgent than the fear
must be the longing to be free

My caring hands will help you
and my watchful eyes will guard you
until the time shall come
to let you go

And we shall meet in freedom
as you find your wings to bear you
high into the sky you had not known
that called you from your prison
that was home

Tremble your glistening wings
called on by love
that sets you free

It Is a Narrow Bridge to Walk

It is a narrow bridge to walk
poised delicately
balanced carefully

moving gently and firmly
out across the raging floods
of buried screaming pain
facing this unmasked danger
with a courage born of love
to reach the other side
and move from death to life
      though not from pain to ease
      or dark to light
It is a healing journey still
      forwards
      onwards
      alone
for all must walk alone
into the forest often dark

yet full of strange mysterious light
that calls me on to walk a way
unknown where demons hide
and angels wait there too

I sense God's presence by a pool so deep
a counterpoint to raging sweeping floods
and wait in stillness
till God's silence and my silence
meet in quiet tenderness
and without a word
God understands my pain
my joy
my wounds
and all my hard long journey to this place

Day passes into night without the need of words

Slowly I rest in quiet peace and sleep
until the gentle dawning of another day
made holy by the presence

of a Self beyond my self
and know so far beyond all knowing
that however far I travel
in solitude and searching
I will feel God come towards me
in the half-light of the evening
and in the moment of that meeting
I shall lift my soul in wonder
at the edge of time and space
and far beyond

Let There be Love
Inspired by Julian of Norwich

God my Maker, you have said, let there be love
and there was love
and in your love you gave me life
    and love and life
      were true
      and beautiful
      and good

God my Keeper, you have said, let there be love
and there were wounds in that love
as you held me close and let me go
      waiting and growing
      disturbing and changing
      holding and freeing
      dying and living
      being and becoming

And love and life were true and beautiful and good
but darkly shadowed
in the hidden depths
that wait your love

God my Lover, you have said, let there be love
and there was joy in that love
and there was pain in that love
        meeting and parting
        movement and stillness
        silence and speaking
        nearness and distance
        summer and winter
        darkness and daylight

And there was wounding in that love
that brought me home
and set me free

A Meditation

When I walk through the valley of the shadow of death...

Psalm 23:4

When the cold dark chill of the night
sears my soul
and the wild beasts prowl
in my heart
You stay with me

And when I am alone unsure
in the darkening forest depths
where none have gone before
and the way within
unclear
and the path beyond
unmarked
You wait with me

With love
You wait
until the sun shines warm

in my soul
and the birds sing loud
in my heart
and I would cry
with the pain
of the joy
of the song
in my soul and my heart

You share with me
creation's hymn
and in this holy place
of joy and pain
You offer me the awesome mystery
of bread and wine

There in the quiet stillness I may hear
the silent sound of angels' wings
where earth meets heaven
and wounds are healed
and I am whole again

Here
where the soft streams run gently
reflecting back a clean pure light
that springs up in my hope-filled heart
and the forest pools rest deep and still
and echo back a solemn mystery
that lives within my waiting soul

Here O my God
You walk with me
and stay with me
and wait with me
and share with me
within the silent stillness
of this solitude
you wait in love
till I am whole again

This Good December Morning

The sun shone
this good December morning
with a golden light
misting the winter trees
with glistening silent tears
that speak of mystery
and sadness
that sees the gentle fabric
of my soul's mysterious depths
both torn and healed again

But this I know
God will not let me go
beyond the range of gentle love
a love mysterious and strong
that angels know

It is a love that does not speak
nor needs to speak

but gives
forever gives
a quiet tender strength
and holds in everlasting trust
the sacred hidden thread
that reaches out
across the space
a space sometimes
all darkness grief and pain
and sings the angels' song
and sees the edge of light
beyond the dark
and hope within my wounded waiting heart
begins to live again

For in the end
a deep and painful angel truth
for those who see the golden light
against the snow touched winter trees
is this

a haunting paradox

  we all must grieve alone
  yet not alone

The Voice of the Holy One

And God spoke in the shadowing cloud
at the edge of space and time
  listen to Him
  listen to Christ

And the disciples were silent
And the preachers and the teachers were silent
And the theologians and the evangelists were silent
And the philosophers and the pastors were silent
And the women and the men and the children
  all were silent

All was stillness and silence
before the awesome mystery
of this transforming light
and the dark shadowing cloud
that stirs a trembling fear

And the voice of the Holy One
is heard

is heard in the street
and the traffic slows and stops
is heard in the fields
and the work slows and stops
eating and drinking
dancing and playing
all slow and stop

For the voice of the Holy One is heard

FINCHALE PRIORY   WED 88

Seeing with the Eye of the Heart

True seeing is to see
not just a dull dead leaf
on a pavement
wet gritty and cold
blown by the casual biting wind
on a bleak November day
cursing the dark
and chilling the soul

But to see
living autumn sepia and gold
and the sharp-edged winter trees
splendid and strong
frosted charcoal black
against the blue-grey purple
of a snow-filled sky

That catches the breath
and starts the tears

and stirs the heart
and touches something deep within
too deep for words
to see
to know
that this should be
and was
and was
and will be

Time on endless time
and far beyond

So who am I
And who are you
and how and why

How may we understand
the awesome mystery
of life and love
and winter trees

and death
and live with grounded hope

It is the very stillness
at the heart of all that is
and my own heart
and yours

It is the air we breathe
without our thinking

It is the touch that joins us
without our asking

It is the beauty that enchants us
without our knowing

It is the driving will that leads us
and our anger at injustice
in our search for peace and wholeness

It is our wonder at the edge of space and time
where answers must elude us

and mystery surrounds us
and death and birth
delight and pain
hope and despair
sorrow and joy
are one
and all is love

God Speaks in the Darkness

When the night
is dark and long my child
and your soul
is stretched to break
your heart
too tired for tears
and your thoughts
too tense to feel

    gently
let me hold you
in the silence of my love
    safely
let me hide you
in the stillness of my peace
    firmly
let me guard you
in the centre of my care

Remember
always remember
when the pain-filled night is dark
and you are far from home
I will go out and search for you
and find you

      and I will stay with you
      always
      I will stay with you
      silent gentle strong

I will reach out across the space
and hold and hide and keep you
in the stillness of my Love

For Here is Peace

Outside
the rain sweeps cold and harsh
across a winter landscape
chill and wet
and nature shivers
as she waits another spring

But in the hidden landscape of my heart
a gentle candle light
is burning soft and warm
and winter darkness
yields to healing peace

For here is peace
a deep and lasting peace
that waits and waits
within the light-filled
nurturing sheltering secret garden of my soul

And here alone in quiet solitude

let faith and hope and love
reach down into my anguished depths
to hold a mirror to that pain

And then and only then
I see within those depths
much more
far more than only mine
where all the pain
of all the world
is held within the heart of One
whose name is Love

Letting Go

The well of healing life
springs from the very heart
of God
whose love can know no bounds
and is not hidden far beyond
the reach of broken wounded hearts
and souls
and does not ask a price
nor seek a love returned

The healing love of God
that hides in every human heart
asks this
and only this
        Let go
        let go of every aching want
        of fierce desire
        of every agonising grasping need
        of all demands and certainties

            of knowledge
            dogma
            safety
            things
            let go of God
            let go of love
and find the love
that reaches far beyond
the bounds of human thought

where faith is sight
and hope is now
and love
unfettered boundless love
is all in all

Journey of the Soul

At the edge
of the forest he waits
where there is no path that he should walk
where there is no sign that he should read

He looks within
to hear the word that calls him
onwards inwards downwards
to the place where no one is
where none have been
nor ever shall
for he must tread this path that he creates
alone
and find himself
in solitude
and darkness
where there is a mystic light
that speaks of wonder
peace and joy

though always
torn with pain

He waits with trembling heart
that knows the terror
of the lonely bleakness
of the night
yet also knows the mystery
of a deeper truth
learned and unlearned
and learned again
that comes with moving on
from dreams and darkness
that have offered life
yet could not
take him on the deepest
inward journey of his soul
Yet without these dreams
and darkness
this journey could not be...

The Healing Time

Disturbing ripples to the surface of my pool
become so soon like surging waves
that crash and thunder
on unyielding rocks
stirring the murky shadowed mud
as in a fiercely driven storm
that threatens
untold darkness fear and pain

But when I stop
and choose to be alone
to find the healing time
to stand back from the pain
to be at one
with who I am
and with the angels
light a gentle candle
in my inner secret soul
and softly calmly

choose to feel the pain
there I am safe
beneath the shadow of their wings
and there in solitude
I wait in hope

A growing peaceful strength
that none can touch
wells up from hidden depths
within that solitude
and I am whole again

I Am a Child Again

I am a child again
young open keen to learn
and all the world and endless time
before me wait

It is the early morning of beginning time
and I must wait the One
who holds the key
to lead me into life and show me love

I am a child
alone inhibited
and loving solitude
quick to withdraw into a secret world
of fantasy
romantic dreams of beauty mystery and love
meet harsh dark fears
that come unasked from hidden depths
with fearful threats

And always at this terrifying edge
dark hidden fears meet mystic love and beauty
yet unknown
Both hold me in disturbing unknown might
and wait the One who robs the fears of power
and frees the love from self-indulgent dreams

I wait for Wisdom in the garden's secret place
where love and fear and fear and love
are interwoven in my heart and in my soul
beyond my mind

Gently she comes
with awesome shadowed light
and takes my hand and draws me
into mysteries beyond the edge of all I know and understand
and leads me into depths
defying images or words

Could I but choose to go in total trust
and follow her whose name is Love
whose way is truth
whose truth is life

For she who played in Eden's garden
at the dawn of cosmic time
and stayed within Gethsemane's dark dread
has found me in my garden's secret place
where all is open known revealed
both crushed and healed by Love

Light a Gentle Candle

William lit many candles as a way of holding in love the people whose lives touched his.

Today
and every day
I need to find a time
to wait in quiet peace

Then from my heart
I take a living flame
and light a gentle candle with my love
and place its healing light
within the souls of those
whose souls touch mine

Today and every day
I hold their darkness and their light
their sorrow and their joy
their peace and their despair

Today
across dividing space

I hold their truth and love
and know that they hold me

Maypole Farm Chapel